A
Chronicle of North Carolina during the American Revolution
1763-1789

Jeffrey J. Crow

Raleigh
Division of Archives and History
North Carolina Department of Cultural Resources

FOREWORD

A Chronicle of North Carolina during the American Revolution, 1763-1789 first appeared in 1975 as part of the bicentennial series North Carolina in the American Revolution. It proved a popular title and soon sold out. Because the bicentennial celebration had ended and the publishing budget remained sparse, the Historical Publications Section allowed the title to remain out of print. Over the years, however, the office has received numerous requests for the booklet. Now the section is delighted once again to include the work among its inventory.

The author of the *Chronicle* is Jeffrey J. Crow, who began a distinguished career in North Carolina as heritage consultant for the North Carolina Bicentennial Committee. Since that appointment, Dr. Crow has become one of the Tar Heel State's premier historians. For a number of years he served as administrator of the Historical Publications Section and editor in chief of the *North Carolina Historical Review*. In 1995 he became director of the North Carolina Division of Archives and History. He is a member and/or officer of various historical organizations and the recipient of several honors and awards. Dr. Crow is the author of a number of articles and books on North Carolina history, including a textbook used in the state's public schools. His *Black Experience in Revolutionary North Carolina*, also published by the Historical Publications Section, has continued in print since the bicentennial and remains much in demand, especially for college and university courses. A native of Akron, Ohio, Dr. Crow holds a Ph.D. degree from Duke University, where he was elected to Phi Beta Kappa.

Joe A. Mobley, *Administrator*

Historical Publications Section
March 1997

Continental Infantryman

Introduction

This pamphlet, designed as a reference work, presents a brief overview of North Carolina in the American Revolution. It examines significant events and developments from the implementation of Great Britain's "new colonial policy" in 1763 to North Carolina's ratification of the federal Constitution in 1789. These dates correspond roughly to an era known as the American Revolution, though some historians have argued that the Revolution antedated 1763, while others have insisted that it scarcely had begun in 1789. North Carolina's place in that epoch has too often been neglected or overlooked. Yet as this "chronicle" demonstrates, revolutionary passions intensified early in North Carolina so that by 1776 the province was in the vanguard of those colonies demanding independence.

North Carolina's experience in the American Revolution subtly contrasted with that of other colonies. North Carolina ranked fourth in population among the thirteen colonies with approximately 265,000 whites and 80,000 blacks in 1775. The colony had been sparsely populated until the mid-eighteenth century when a rapid influx of new settlers and immigrants occurred. The new immigration brought great numbers of Scotch-Irish, Germans, Scots Highlanders, Welsh, English, and Africans to North Carolina. The overwhelming majority of North Carolinians were farmers. A small number resided in hamlets and towns along major rivers. Unlike neighboring South Carolina and Virginia, North Carolina never developed an extensive gentry class. The colonial aristocracy that existed revolved around the older families of the Albemarle and Cape Fear regions. Few of the gentry owned over fifty slaves; most held less than twenty. Yeoman farmers generally owned no slaves, and indentured servitude—"Christian servants"—had all but disappeared by the time of the Revolution. Nor were all Negroes bondsmen. The number of free Negroes in the colony increased steadily, if slowly, so that by 1790 as many as 5,000 blacks remained free, despite legal stipulations that they must leave North Carolina. Most free blacks were farmers, though a considerable number had no doubt earned their freedom by hiring out their services as artisans. Indians too dotted the colony. As many as 35,000 Indians, representing thirty tribes, had lived in North Carolina at one time, but by the middle of the eighteenth century considerably fewer probably remained.

With the rapid population increase after 1750 had come sharper sectional and social tensions. The new settlers in the backcountry demanded greater representation in the colonial assembly which the eastern counties, jealous of their powers and prerogatives, were reluctant to grant. Such tensions helped spawn the War of Regulation (1768-1771) which pitted North Carolinian against North Carolinian at a time when other colonists were focusing their wrath on Great Britain. Conflict existed too between the so-called "popular party" which stood for colonial rights and the followers of the royal governors who upheld the powers of Britain and the crown.

It was in this context, then, that North Carolina entered the Revolutionary period. Through a network of extra legal institutions such as committees of safety and provincial congresses, North Carolinians erected a new state government, raised a militia and army, dealt with dissenting internal elements, levied taxes, and prosecuted a war. During three decades of turmoil, the colony suffered a bitter schism within its own citizenry. Unlike most other colonies, North Carolina had an unusually large and active tory population which loyally continued to support the mother country after patriots, or whigs as they were known, had taken the first halting steps toward revolution by defying king and parliament. Civil warfare between tory and whig partisans, brutally evident at the Battle of Moore's Creek Bridge in 1776, did not abate until 1782, months after Lord Charles Cornwallis's legendary pursuit of Nathanael Greene through North Carolina. Between 1776 and 1780, North Carolina escaped the devastation of war on her own soil. But in the last climactic stages of the Revolutionary War, the Tar Heel state became the scene of Greene's skillful retreat before Cornwallis's crack British regulars. The Battle of Guilford Court House ravaged the British forces and led to Cornwallis's celebrated surrender at Yorktown.

After the war, North Carolina proved intractable toward ratification of the federal Constitution. Long a bastion of antifederalism, North Carolina was the next to last state to approve the Constitution and join the United States. The depth and strength of antifederalism reflected the small farmer constituency of the state which distrusted congressional and executive power. Though Antifederalist leaders tended to own slightly less property than their Federalist counterparts, the difference was not so pronounced or wide as to explain North Carolina's obstinacy strictly in terms of class. Rather the geography, economy, and society of the state had traditionally decentralized the political structure thereby providing North Carolina with a certain degree of insulation from developments in other parts of the nation.

Still North Carolina's diverse experiences in the American Revolution have given its people a rich and proud heritage. Tory or whig, Federalist or Antifederalist, North Carolinians fought, bled, and died for cherished principles which helped shape the American Revolution and the new nation.

The author wishes to acknowledge a debt of gratitude to the historians listed in the bibliography from whose works so much of this pamphlet was collated.

J.J.C.   Raleigh, North Carolina 1975

A Chronicle. . .

1763 October 7

Initiating a "new colonial policy" and attempting to defuse Indian warfare on the western frontier, the British government implemented the Proclamation Line. The Great War for the Empire, or French and Indian War as it was known in North America, had depleted Great Britain's treasury. Consequently, a new policy of taxation in conjunction with the Proclamation Line was inaugurated. Prior to 1763, the colonies had been subject to a system of Navigation Acts ostensibly controlling their trade and industry. But these acts had been widely ignored and loosely enforced. The Proclamation Line was to serve as a western boundary for all the colonies including North Carolina. The Moravians, a German religious sect on the western fringes of the colony, noted that the new boundary would favor the Indians more than the settlers. For the most part, however, the Proclamation Line was ignored as North Carolina frontiersmen like Daniel Boone explored deeper into the continent's interior. More portentous was a new taxation policy which could not be so easily ignored.

1764 October 31

The initial taxes levied on the colonies under the "new colonial policy" had little direct effect in North Carolina. The Sugar and Currency Acts of 1764 aroused heated opposition in other colonies, but North Carolina found them to be minor irritants. Even so, North Carolinians recognized the threat to "home-rule" or self-government posed by the British Parliament's new tax policy. On this date the lower house of the General Assembly expressed its outrage over the Sugar Act to Governor Arthur Dobbs. The legislators denounced the "new Taxes and Impositions laid on us without our Privilege and Consent" and claimed that the right of taxation was reserved to the General Assembly of the colony, not to the British Parliament. Such a stern denunciation presaged the more violent reaction that would accompany the Stamp Act.

1765 October 19

The infamous Stamp Act, passed by the Parliament in March, 1765, offended many colonists who resented direct taxation without their consent. Under the act, legal documents, bills of lading, newspapers, pamphlets, almanacs, dice, playing cards, and other such items had to carry stamps. Actually the tax was less than similar ones levied in England, and the revenues were to be spent only on the defense of the North American colonies. The colonists, however, viewed the Stamp Act otherwise, and reaction to it was swift and violent.

On this date some 500 people in the Lower Cape Fear region gathered near Wilmington to stage a demonstration against the new tax. They hanged Lord Bute in effigy, built a huge bonfire, went from house to house seeking more revelers, and caroused well into the night with toasts to "Liberty, Property, and No Stamp Duty." It was probably on this occasion that the Cape Fear region formed its Sons of Liberty, a group of firebrands who consistently opposed the encroachments of king and parliament on the colonies. Similar demonstrations took place that autumn in New Bern, Cross Creek, and Edenton.

Cape Fear Patriots Resist the Landing of Stamps at Brunswick

1765 October 31

The Lower Cape Fear continued to be the hotbed of resistance to the Stamp Act as a second demonstration occurred on Halloween night. Fires and effigies were again present. This time, however, it was determined that the effigy of Liberty, once thought to be dead, had in fact survived. Placing the effigy in a comfortable armchair, the Wilmington crowd celebrated Liberty's new vitality with a round of toasts and taunts at British authority.

1765 November 16

Resistance to the Stamp Act grew uglier as the Sons of Liberty in Wilmington escorted Dr. William Houston, the newly appointed stamp agent for the Lower Cape Fear, to the courthouse. Before a mob of some three or four hundred protestors of the Stamp Act, and with drums beating and flags streaming, Dr. Houston was forced to resign his commission. Liquor flowed freely, and Liberty placards adorned the hats of the Sons of Liberty. They extorted a pledge from the editor of the *North Carolina Gazette* to publish his paper without the required stamps. When the newspaper appeared, a legend across its margin and just above a skull and crossbones declared, "This is the place to affix the Stamp."

1765 November 18

Alarmed by the accelerating movement against the Stamp Act, North Carolina's new royal governor, the shrewd William Tryon, called a meeting with the patriot leaders of the Cape Fear region. Some fifty merchants and planters dined with Tryon. The governor urged the leaders to permit the circulation of the stamps. Tryon claimed that he himself opposed the Stamp Act, but until the law was repealed, it must be enforced. He even promised to obtain an exemption for North Carolina. The next morning the leaders firmly rejected the governor's plea on the grounds that to permit the operation of the act would be to acknowledge Parliament's right to tax the colonies, a right that the patriot leaders refused to concede.

1765 November 29

An armed body of men led by such Wilmington whigs as Hugh Waddell and John Ashe refused to permit the landing of stamps at Brunswick. The stamps had arrived on the British ship *Diligence*. In retaliation Governor Tryon placed a ban on all transactions in the courts. The result was a stalemate over the next few weeks and a stoppage of business and trade.

1766 February 18

A meeting of the Cape Fear leaders was held in Wilmington at which an "Association" was formed to prevent the execution of the Stamp Act. The signers vowed to resist the Stamp Act even if it meant risking their lives and fortunes. The British tax was termed "subversive of the Liberties and Charters of North America." Among the signers were John Ashe, Hugh Waddell, and Cornelius Harnett.

1766 February 19-21

The day after the Association was signed, an armed mob of hundreds marched from Wilmington to Brunswick to demand the release of two ships seized by the British because their clearance papers had not been stamped. After posting a guard around Governor Tryon's house, the mob broke into the customs office and stole the papers of the seized vessels. By February 20, nearly one thousand men had gathered in Brunswick. Emboldened by their numbers, the patriots boarded a British ship which had detained the merchant vessels and coerced the captain into releasing the ships. Thereafter vessels entered and cleared the Cape Fear without challenge and without stamps.

Still not satisfied, the armed mob surrounded Governor Tryon's residence on February 21 and demanded that William Pennington, comptroller of customs, give himself up. At first Tryon refused, while Pennington, so the legend goes, hid under the governor's bed. In a confrontation between Tryon and Cornelius Harnett, "the Samuel Adams of North Carolina," the whig leader warned that if Pennington did not come out, then the people would take him by force. The governor and Pennington yielded. Accompanied by the mob, Pennington went to the center of town and along with other officials swore not to execute the Stamp Act. Indeed, the harried Pennington resigned his post.

Thus, the Sons of Liberty successfully resisted the Stamp Act. The protestors had been led by gentlemen, planters, and merchants. The threat of mob violence and even rebellion throughout the colonies had compelled the British to back down, for Parliament soon repealed the Stamp Act. But the will of the American colonies to resist taxation and to stand united would be tested again quickly as new British taxes were forthcoming. Indeed, the Declaratory Act, passed in March, 1766, clearly asserted Parliament's right to tax the colonies, but American whigs, buoyed by their recent success, chose to ignore it.

1768 November 11

In 1767 Parliament adopted the Townshend Act which placed import duties on wine, tea, paper, glass, and lead. Because the duties were intended to pay the salaries of colonial governors and judges, and because the taxes fell most heavily on the commercial colonies, strident opposition arose immediately. Over the years the power of the purse had come to reside with the lower houses of assembly in the colonies which paid the salaries of public officials and even the governors. The Townshend Act, among other things, threatened that important power.

On November 11, 1768, the North Carolina General Assembly, led by Speaker of the House John Harvey, offered an address to the king. Couched in conciliatory but firm language, the petition expressed loyalty to the king but condemned the Townshend Act as illegal and unconstitutional. Declaring the duty an infringement on North Carolinians' constitutional rights as British citizens, the legislators asserted: "Free men cannot legally be taxed but by themselves or their representatives. . . ." In their view, Parliament did not represent North Carolina. They did.

9

1769 November 2

When the General Assembly convened in October, 1769, the Townshend Act remained in force. John Harvey presented the legislature a copy of the Virginia resolutions of non-importation. When the lower house adopted the resolutions without a dissenting vote, Governor Tryon dissolved the assembly. Undeterred by the governor's maneuver, Harvey called a meeting of the assemblymen at the New Bern courthouse. With Harvey acting as moderator, a convention of sixty-four of the sixty-seven legislators met for two days. The extralegal convention adopted a "non-importation association," which was to become effective on January 1, 1770. No slaves, wine, or British manufactures of any kind were to be imported.

In March, 1770, the Parliament repealed all the taxes, save the one on tea. The Townshend duties had not produced the revenue that had been anticipated. They only brought bitter opposition on both sides of the Atlantic.

1770 June 2

On this date the Wilmington patriots summoned a meeting of the Sons of Liberty. Under the leadership of James Moore and Cornelius Harnett, a committee was selected to enforce and maintain the non-importation policy and to cooperate with sister colonies even though the Townshend Act had been abrogated. Just how effective the boycott was cannot be determined. Writing to England in 1771, Governor Tryon insisted that the non-importation policy had been a failure despite the "boasted associations of people who never were in trade, and the sham patriotism of a few merchants to the southward of the province. . . ." In any event, colonial resistance to British authority had once again forced Parliament to lift every tax except the one on tea, and that bittersweet herb would soon play a pivotal role in the colonies' destiny.

Governor Tryon and the Regulators

1771 May 16

The Battle of Alamance climaxed over a decade of social unrest, violence, and disorder in the backcountry. Known as the Regulation, the volatile movement protested the corruption of government officials who were charging extortionate fees for land claims and similar legal proceedings. Governor Tryon estimated that county sheriffs, who by law were the tax collectors, had embezzled over half the tax money due the colonial government between 1754 and 1767. Specie or coin was already scarce in the backcountry, and the regulators found little sympathy for their grievances in the General Assembly which drew its strength and leadership from the East.

At first the regulators had tried to present their case in a peaceful manner. Many refused to pay their taxes. Disorders soon followed, however, as the regulators harassed public officials and assaulted others. In 1770 amid rumors that the regulators were going to march on the legislature in New Bern, Samuel Johnston, the conservative whig from Edenton, drafted the so-called "Riot" or "Bloody Act." This law permitted prosecutions for rioting to take place in any county even though the disturbance did not occur there; it also declared as outlaws any persons refusing arrest. Most importantly, it authorized Governor Tryon to quell the Regulation by military force if necessary.

With the imprimatur of the legislature, then, Governor Tryon decided on a dramatic and severe course of action. Calling up the colonial militia, he marched into the heart of regulator country—Orange County—and met a large force of rebels near Alamance Creek. In a two-hour battle, the militia inflicted a bloody defeat on the regulators. Six of their leaders were later hanged in Hillsborough.

Ironically, Tryon had won the full support of the eastern whigs in quashing the Regulation. Many of the men who later performed prominent roles in the Revolutionary War, and who had already led resistance to the Stamp and Townshend Acts, fought at Alamance. Among them were James Moore, Richard Caswell, Alexander Lillington, Robert Howe, and John Ashe. Other whigs like Cornelius Harnett and Samuel Johnston had sponsored harsh sanctions against the regulators in the assembly.

When the break with Great Britain came several years later, these eastern whigs had reason to wonder if the backcountry— the scene of the Regulation—would support the revolutionary cause. And what of the regulators themselves? Were they part of the revolutionary ferment of the period? If one accepts Carl Becker's thesis that the American Revolution was twofold—a struggle for home-rule and for who would rule at home—then the regulators fit into a larger pattern of conflict throughout the colonies that existed between coastal and backcountry sections. In seeking a better government to redress their grievances and in challenging a royal governor and eastern-dominated legislature unresponsive to their needs, the regulators clearly stood for principles which stirred revolutionaries throughout the colonies.

1773 March 6

One of the key local issues that propelled North Carolina into the rising tide of revolution was the clash between the governor and the legislature over the colony's court system. This conflict came to a head in the years immediately preceding the Revolutionary War.

The lower house had regularly exercised the right to attach the property of foreigners in debt to North Carolinians. But in 1772 the crown issued instructions to all royal governors that they were not to assent to any bills that attached the property of people who had never lived in the colonies. In March, 1773, the North Carolina superior court bill expired, and the lower house, ignoring the crown's directives, prepared a new superior court bill that once again included an attachment clause. Governor Josiah Martin, who had succeeded Tryon when the latter became governor of New York in 1771, had to reject the bill. However, to insure that the colony had a judicial system, he created courts of oyer and terminer solely by executive fiat, that is, without approval of the legislature. He appointed Maurice Moore and Richard Caswell, along with Chief Justice Martin Howard, as judges of the new courts. The governor's move infuriated the General Assembly which interpreted the new courts as a flagrant challenge to its judicial powers.

1773 December 4

When the new legislature met in December, 1773, it refused to appropriate funds for the governor's courts and denied his right to create such courts without the "aid of the Legislature of this Province." Nor would the assembly pass a superior court law without the foreign attachment clause. An impasse had been reached. Governor Martin prorogued the assembly for three months, but not before the legislature had appointed North Carolina's first Committee of Correspondence.

In March, 1773, Virginia had inaugurated a Committee of Correspondence and Inquiry to obtain information about all British activities that affected the colonies and to disseminate such information. North Carolina followed Virginia's lead and organized a committee consisting of John Harvey, Robert

Howe, Richard Caswell, Edward Vail, John Ashe, Joseph Hewes, and Samuel Johnston. Committees of Correspondence throughout the colonies signaled an emerging network of revolutionary institutions which were to prove vital to the success of the movement for independence.

1774 March 2

When the General Assembly reconvened in March, 1774, its position on the foreign attachment clause had hardened even more. The situation was more acute than three months earlier, for Martin's courts of oyer and terminer, having been denied funds by the legislature, were no longer functioning. When the legislature passed another superior court bill with the attachment clause, Governor Martin once again rejected it. Fortunately, the governor and the assembly did agree on an inferior court bill and on a bill establishing the courts of oyer and terminer. The latter bill represented a significant concession on the part of the governor, for it implicitly recognized the right of the lower house to approve the establishment of any courts. Even so, North Carolina was left with only a partial judiciary system until the formation of a revolutionary state government nearly three years later. No other grievance, save parliamentary taxation, exercised North Carolinians as much as the controversy over the court system and thus promoted revolutionary sentiment.

1774 June 10

In 1773 the Lord North ministry came to the aid of the East India Company by passing the Tea Act. This act gave the company a monopoly on the tea trade in the colonies and provoked a strong protest from New Hampshire to Georgia. The most celebrated resistance to the Tea Act was the Boston Tea Party in December, 1773. The Parliament, determined to safeguard its authority, enacted the Boston Port Bill and other so-called Coercive Acts which closed the city's port on June 1, 1774.

The Committees of Correspondence swiftly spread the news of Britain's "Intolerable Acts." In June, 1774, the North Carolina committee learned from its Virginia counterpart of the latest sanctions against Boston and of the rapidly building demand for a general congress of all the colonies. Relaying the information to South Carolina, the North Carolina committee expressed its support for a general congress and urged the colonies to stand united against British oppression of Boston. The North Carolinians proposed a boycott of all trade with Britain so long as the port of Boston remained closed. Matching action with its rhetoric, North Carolina sent nearly 2,100 bushels of corn and other commodities to the beleaguered Massachusetts patriots.

1774 July 21

When the Massachusetts legislature issued a formal call for a general congress of the colonies, Governor Josiah Martin refused to summon the North Carolina General Assembly so that it could elect delegates to the proposed congress in Philadelphia. At a mass meeting in Wilmington on July 21, William Hooper, Cornelius Harnett, and others called for a "provincial congress independent of the governor" in order to discuss the continuing difficulties with Britain. The extralegal meeting was eventually set for New Bern, as the cause of Boston became the "common cause of British America."

1774 August 13

Governor Martin issued a proclamation in which he severely chastised the North Carolina whigs for calling an illegal assembly. He commanded the citizens of North Carolina to prevent any further provincial congresses. Nevertheless, a total of seventy-one delegates, representing thirty of thirty-six counties and four of six borough towns, were elected to North Carolina's First Provincial Congress.

1774 August 25

The First Provincial Congress met in New Bern and remained in session for three days with John Harvey serving as moderator. The extralegal assembly swept North Carolina into the mainstream of revolution. While professing loyalty to the crown,

A Proclamation

Whereas it appears to me, that, meetings and Assemblies of the Inhabitants of this Province have been in some of the Counties and Towns thereof already held, and are in others appointed to be held without any Legal authority; and that resolves have been entered into and plans concerted (in such meetings as are passed;) derogatory to his Majesty and the Parliament of Great Britain; and that there is reason to apprehend, the same inflammatory, disloyal and indecent, measures, may be adopted in such future assemblies, inconsistent with the Peace and good order of this Government and tending to excite clamour and Discontent among His Majesty's Subjects in this Province; I have thought fit with the advice and consent of His Majesty's Council, to issue this Proclamation, to discourage as much as possible proceedings so illegall and unwarrantable, in their nature, and in their effect, so obviously injurious to the welfare of this Country; And to this end I do hereby strictly require and enjoin, on their allegience, all and every His Majesty's Subjects, to forbear to attend at any such illegal meetings, and that they do discourage and prevent the same by all and every means in their power, and more particularly that they do forbear to attend, and do prevent as far as in them lies, the meeting of certain Deputies, said to be appointed to be held at NewBern on the 25th Instant. An I do more especially charge, require and Command, all and every His Majesty's Justices of the Peace, Shreiffs and other officers, to be aiding and assisting herein to the utmost of their Power.

Given under my Hand and the Great Seal of the said Province at NewBern the 13th day of August 1774 and in the fourteenth Year of His Majesty's Reign.

God save The King

Jo. Martin

Governor Martin's Proclamation, August 13, 1774.

the assembly took a vigorous stand against parliamentary taxation which it considered "illegal and oppressive." The assembly also endorsed a general congress and economic boycott of trade with Britain, while pledging support to Boston. William Hooper, Joseph Hewes, and Richard Caswell were appointed delegates to the First Continental Congress. Furthermore, steps were taken to sustain the revolutionary impetus in North Carolina. The congress authorized John Harvey to summon another provincial congress at his own discretion, and it recommended the establishment of five-member committees of safety in each county. These revolutionary institutions were to act as agencies for the enforcement of the boycott and as committees of correspondence. The First Provincial Congress demonstrated the strength and cohesion of the North Carolina whigs in defying British authority and in uniting with other colonies.

1774 October 25

Legend has it that on this date a group of fifty-one women from at least five counties met at the home of Mrs. Elizabeth King and staged the "Edenton Tea Party." While Mrs. Penelope Barker presided, the ladies signed an "Association" which pledged them to support North Carolina's provincial congress. The Edenton ladies also promised not to drink tea or to wear British manufactures. In Wilmington a similar tea party took place in March, 1775, at which the ladies burned their tea "in solemn procession."

1775 February 11

The First Continental Congress had met in Philadelphia in September and October, 1774, to fashion a stronger colonial union, safeguard colonial rights, and implement the boycott of trade with Great Britain. Within a year trade between England and the colonies declined dramatically by 97 per cent. North Carolina was no exception as British imports fell to a fraction of what they had been.

As the meeting of the Second Continental Congress approached, tensions between Britain and the colonies grew. In February, 1775, John Harvey issued a call for the Second Pro-

Edenton Tea Party Viewed by the London Press

vincial Congress in North Carolina in order to elect delegates to the general congress once again.

1775 March 6

To thwart the Second Provincial Congress in North Carolina, Governor Josiah Martin issued a proclamation urging the people to eschew the illegal assembly. Then in a bold counter-stroke he summoned the legislature to convene in New Bern on April 4. Harvey had designated April 3 as the meeting of the Second Provincial Congress in New Bern. It was Martin's hope that North Carolinians would support the lawful meeting of the colonial assembly instead of the extralegal provincial congress.

1775 April 3

The two bodies that assembled in New Bern in April, 1775, were nearly identical in composition. John Harvey served as moderator of the provincial congress and speaker of the house in the legislature. Indeed, the colonial assembly invited the provincial congress to unite with it, and so the two bodies became one convention. Thoroughly disgusted by the proceedings, Governor Martin repudiated both bodies which in turn denounced Martin. The Second Provincial Congress nonetheless continued the revolutionary impulse by again appointing Hewes, Hooper, and Caswell to the Second Continental Congress, endorsing committees of safety, and creating a Council of Safety for the whole colony. Governor Martin, rather than countenance such irregular activities, dissolved the legislature on April 8. Thus the last royal assembly that ever met in North Carolina came to an end. But steps to form a new revolutionary government had been taken.

1775 May 20

Tradition has it that the Mecklenburg Committee of Safety met on this date in Charlotte and drafted a "Declaration of Independence." Because the original minutes were burned and the statement was later written from memory by John McKnitt Alexander, historians have long disputed the authenticity of the Mecklenburg Declaration of Independence. No question, however, surrounds the Mecklenburg Resolves which were adopted at a meeting in Charlotte on May 31, 1775. These resolves declared "null and void" all commissions granted by the king and further urged the citizens of Mecklenburg to elect military officers whose powers would be "independent" of the mother country. In the wake of the clashes at Lexington and Concord, Massachusetts, the revolutionary movement in North Carolina, as manifest in such military preparations, was taking an ominous turn.

Abner Nash

1775 May 23

Led by Abner Nash, a "motley mob" of patriots marched on the governor's palace in New Bern to protest the dismounting of the cannon in the palace yard. Angry at and alarmed by recent developments, Governor Martin had tried to hide the cannon for fear that the New Bern Committee of Safety would seize them. In fact, that was precisely what Nash and his compatriots had in mind. Martin explained to the whig leader that the cannon were being repaired. His efforts were to no avail, however, for the New Bern patriots, purportedly "stimulated by liquor," carried off the remaining cannon.

1775 May 31

Revolution seemed to be in the air everywhere in North Carolina on this date. Besides the Mecklenburg Resolves, the New Bern Committee of Safety also expressed North Carolina's new sense of independence. The committee drew up an "Association" which, while ostensibly loyal to the crown, declared the whigs' intent to oppose England's "wicked" ministries. Calling for a union of all the colonies, the New Bern patriots pledged their support to the Continental Congress, thereby recognizing in effect the extralegal authority of the general congress as being above that of king and parliament.

It was also on this date that Josiah Martin became the first royal governor in the colonies to flee his office. Amid rumors that the New Bern Committee of Safety would seize the palace, Martin departed for Fort Johnston at the mouth of the Cape Fear River. His flight marked the demise of royal authority in North Carolina. Henceforth, the North Carolina whigs would assume responsibility for affairs of state in the province and the establishment of new governmental institutions. As war clouds gathered in the North, North Carolinians set about the task of forming a new provisional government.

1775 June 19

Charging that "North Carolina alone remains an inactive Spectator of this general defensive Armament," the North Carolina delegates to the Continental Congress — Hewes, Hooper, and Caswell — implored the county and town committees of safety to support the revolutionary movement, for the "fate of Boston was the common fate of all." Striking a militant chord, the colony's delegates urged North Carolina to boycott all trade with England and to deprive the powerful British navy of the colony's indispensable naval stores. "We conjure you," the impassioned delegates declared, "by the Ties of Religion Virtue and Love of your Country to follow the Example of your sister Colonies and to form yourselves into a Militia." Exhorting the committees to study the martial arts, store gunpowder, and save ammunition, the delegates intoned gravely, "the Crisis of America is not at a great distance."

William Hooper

Joseph Hewes

1775 July 13

The General Assembly was scheduled to convene at New Bern on July 12, but Governor Martin, having taken refuge on the British ship *Cruizer*, prorogued the body until September 12 and then later decided not to call it at all.

John Harvey had died in May, so responsibility for summoning a new provincial congress had fallen to the cautious and conservative Samuel Johnston of Edenton. Johnston received many petitions urging him to call another congress. The Wilmington Committee of Safety perhaps outlined the most compelling reasons for holding another congress. "Our situation here is truly alarming," the Wilmington patriots wrote Johnston on July 13, "the Governor collecting men, provisions, warlike stores of every kind, spiriting up the back counties, and perhaps the Slaves, finally strengthening the fort with new works, in such a manner as may make the Capture of it extremely difficult. In this Situation, Sir, our people are Continually clamoring for a provincial Convention. They hope every thing from its Immediate Session, fear every thing from its delay." Whether a new congress met or not, the Wilmington whigs were prepared to act.

1775 July 19

Some 500 militia and minutemen, led by Cornelius Harnett, John Ashe, and Robert Howe, took possession of Fort Johnston on the Lower Cape Fear. The Wilmington Committee of Safety had organized and coordinated the attack on the fort, where the patriots hoped to capture British artillery and other supplies. But the cannon had been spiked. Determined to prevent future British occupation, the whig force burned the fort to the ground. Governor Martin blamed the troubles on the "evil, pernicious and traiterous councils and . . . seditious committees" and their "atrocious leaders." North Carolina, allaying earlier whig fears, had now entered into armed rebellion against the mother country.

1775 August 8

Governor Martin, warning the people not to support the Third Provincial Congress, issued his famous "Fiery Proclamation." Martin ascribed the colony's woes to the treasonous and inflammatory committees of safety. Denouncing the July attack on Fort Johnston, the royal governor also damned the Mecklenburg Resolves and the confiscation of the palace cannon by the New Bern committee. Such conduct, he asserted, was "subversive of His Majesty's Government." Though he believed that the majority of North Carolinians remained loyal to the crown, Martin insisted that another provincial congress could "bring the Affairs of this Country to a Crisis...."

1775 August 20

A total of 184 delegates, representing every county and town, gathered at Hillsborough for the Third Provincial Congress. The delegates signed a "test oath" which expressed allegiance to the crown but denied the right of Parliament to tax the colonies. Recognizing that there were significant numbers of North Carolinians who might oppose the whig cause, the congress appointed committees to confer with the Scots Highlanders who had recently arrived in the colony and with the old regulators. Displaying a certain measure of caution, and perhaps reflecting the conservative views of its presiding officer, Samuel Johnston, the assembly rejected Benjamin Franklin's proposal — suggested at the Continental Congress — for a colonial confederation. Such a plan, it was believed, might injure chances for reconciliation with the mother country.

Even so, North Carolinians made firm strides toward independence. The congress replied to Governor Martin's "Fiery Proclamation" by denouncing his desertion of the colony. In an address to the people of North Carolina, the delegates announced that they would establish a temporary government for the peace and stability of the province. Moreover, they insisted that the people were bound by the acts and resolutions of the Continental and Provincial Congresses because "in both they are freely represented by persons chosen by themselves." Instituting a provisional government, the congress divided North Carolina into six military districts and made arrangements for a provincial congress and provincial council that would act as the chief executive and administrative agency in the colony. Local government was to be based on the existing system of safety committees. To fund the new government, the congress issued its own provincial currency which was to be floated on the collection of all back taxes and on a poll tax which would commence in 1777 and continue for nine years. Social ostracism and harsh penalties were promised to those who refused to honor the colony's new currency.

The boldest actions taken by the congress concerned preparations for war. Accusing Governor Martin of conspiring to weaken North Carolina's unity with her sister colonies, the delegates placed the colony in a "state of defence." The congress authorized the formation of two regiments of 500 men each for the Continental Line and named James Moore and Robert Howe the commanding colonels. Provisions were also made for six battalions of militia. By placing North Carolina on a war footing, the Third Provincial Congress had readied the colony for the ultimate consequences of revolution.

1775 December 14

North Carolina's military preparations were soon tested, not on her home soil, but in Virginia and South Carolina. Late in 1775, Virginia asked North Carolina for military assistance against royal governor, Lord Dunmore, who with British regulars had initiated a campaign of burning houses, plundering plantations, and seizing slaves. In fact, Dunmore issued a proclamation emancipating all slaves who joined the British forces.

North Carolina whigs heeded the pleas of their Virginia counterparts and sent troops to Norfolk, where they helped to defeat the British at the Battle of Great Bridge. The British were driven from Norfolk.

1775 December 22

In South Carolina, meanwhile, the whigs were faced by a large group of loyalists, known as the "Scovellites." Coming to the aid of the patriot cause in South Carolina, the North Carolina Line helped to crush the tories in the "Snow Campaign," so named because it was fought during a freakish snow storm. At home, however, an even more dangerous threat from the tories loomed.

1776 January 10

John Adams once wrote that "nearly one third of the people of the colonies" were loyal to the crown in the sense that before 1775 the British had "seduced and deluded" that number of Americans. In North Carolina an unusually large and active number of loyalists not only supported Britain but took up arms against their whig brethren.

Governor Martin played upon the breach within the North Carolina citizenry and hoped to quash the whigs by appealing to the loyalist segment of the colony's population. In January, 1776, he issued another proclamation calling upon the king's "faithful subjects" to rally to the royal standard. Proclaiming all who refused "Rebels and Traitors," Martin empowered the tory leaders in North Carolina to raise an army and march to Brunswick.

Martin had devised a four-point plan to crush the whig rebellion in North Carolina. First, he expected to raise an indigenous army of some three thousand Highland Scots, three thousand regulators, and another three thousand tories. Second, Lord Charles Cornwallis was to bring seven regiments of British regulars to North Carolina. Third, Sir Peter Parker would accompany Cornwallis with a fleet of fifty-four ships. And, finally, Sir Henry Clinton was to bring two thousand seasoned and crack British troops from Boston. All these forces were to rendezvous at Brunswick no later than February 15, 1776.

1776 February 27

With the shadow of war hanging over the province, the North Carolina whigs mobilized their forces to repel an expected British invasion and to interdict a more menacing threat from within. Militia units from Dobbs, Johnston, Pitt, and Craven counties were called out and organized. Two regiments in the North Carolina Line, under the leadership of Colonels Robert Howe and James Moore, made preparations to resist the anticipated attack by the British. Wilmington was put under martial law, and some twenty suspected tories seized and detained.

By mid-February a formidable force of some 1,600 Highland Scots, led by Donald McDonald, had reached Cross Creek in their march from the Piedmont toward the coast. Colonel James Moore, commander of the whig forces, was determined to prevent the loyalists from capturing Wilmington.

In a series of cunning maneuvers, Moore deployed the whig troops, numbering perhaps 1,100, at Moore's Creek Bridge, where they were under the immediate command of Richard Caswell and Alexander Lillington. To reach Wilmington the tory forces would have to cross at that bridge. On the morning of February 27, the whig and loyalist armies clashed in a short but brutally decisive engagement. The whigs had removed many of the planks from the floor of the bridge and greased the log sleepers with soap and tallow. As the Highlanders tried to negotiate the sabotaged bridge, they were raked by a murderous fusillade. The carnage was savage. While the whigs lost only one killed and one wounded, the tories suffered about fifty killed and wounded in a battle that lasted only three minutes. Some 850 tories, including Donald McDonald, were eventually captured along with thousands of weapons and £ 15,000 in gold.

The Battle of Moore's Creek Bridge frustrated British plans to invade North Carolina. When Cornwallis, Parker, and Clinton arrived in May, 1776, they found a dyspeptic Governor Martin and no tory force to welcome them. Turning to Charleston, South Carolina, they left North Carolina free from invasion for the next four years.

After the battle, enthusiasm for the whig cause intensified in the colony and prompted the calling of the Fourth Provincial Congress. But the victory also led to some serious miscalculations about the efficacy of the militia, and the boundless faith in the minutemen later proved misplaced. That overconfidence made it difficult thereafter to maintain a regular army in North Carolina. Still, the Battle of Moore's Creek Bridge accelerated the movement toward independence.

When the Fourth Provincial Congress convened at Halifax in April, 1776, independence was uppermost in the minds of the delegates. Robert Howe, surveying the delegates' views on independence, declared that he knew "not one dissenting voice." A committee of seven, headed by Cornelius Harnett, considered the "usurpations and violences attempted and committed by the King and Parliament" as well as measures for the "better defence of this Province."

On April 12, Harnett's committee submitted a report that was unanimously adopted by the convention. Known as the Halifax Resolves, the report urged the Continental Congress to proclaim independence, negotiate foreign alliances, and reserve to North Carolina "the sole and exclusive right of forming a Constitution and laws for this Colony. . . ." The Halifax Resolves have been termed "the first official *state* action for independence," and other colonies soon followed North Carolina's example.

While the Fourth Provincial Congress also issued more bills of credit to be redeemed by the poll tax and made further provisions for maintaining an army and equipping it, the problem of drafting a state constitution consumed much of the assembly's energies. The whigs, who had proven to be a cohesive force in the movement for independence, began to split into factions over the nature and structure of the new government. Finally, the congress decided not to adopt a state constitution and appointed a Council of Safety to govern the colony until the next congress met. Consisting of nine members, the Council of Safety handled affairs of state—principally military and financial problems—during the critical months of 1776. Cornelius Harnett, the council's president, in effect became ex-officio governor.

The Halifax Congress adjourned on May 15, 1776, after a long and fruitful session. A year earlier, certain North Carolina whigs had feared that the colony lacked the zeal of Massachusetts or Virginia. Now North Carolina stood at the forefront of those colonies advocating independence.

North Carolina   In Congress 12ᵗʰ April 1776

                    The Select Committee to take into
Consideration the Usurpations and Violences attempted and
Committed by the King and Parliament of Britain against
America, and the further measures to be taken for frustrating
the same, and for the better defence of this province, reported
as follows, towit.

                    - It appears to your Committee that pursuantly
to the plan concerted by the British Ministry for subjugating
America, the King and Parliament of Great Britain have
usurped a power over the persons and properties of the
people unlimited and uncontrouled. And disregarding
their humble petitions for peace Liberty and Safety, have
made divers Legislative Acts denouncing War, Famine
and every Species of Calamity against the Continent
in General. That British Fleets and Armies have been
and still are daily employed in destroying the people,
and committing the most horid devastations on the
Country. ——————
                                              That

Halifax Resolves, April 12, 1776

1776 May 5

In accord with Governor Martin's proposed invasion of North Carolina, British General Henry Clinton arrived from Boston and conducted raids along the Lower Cape Fear with the able assistance of Lord Cornwallis. But with no tory army to greet him, Clinton soon withdrew to Charleston, South Carolina, and laid plans for an attack on that colony. Before he did, however, he issued an ultimatum to the whigs of North Carolina. If they did not cease resistance to the crown's sovereignty, grievous consequences would follow, he promised. In a gesture of compromise, Clinton even offered amnesty to all rebels who laid down their arms with two notable exceptions—Cornelius Harnett and Robert Howe of Wilmington. Clinton's warning went unheeded.

1776 June 28

Their plans to invade North Carolina thwarted, the British attacked Fort Moultrie in Charleston harbor. Whig forces, however, proved equal to the task as they repelled the British assault. Under the command of Colonel Robert Howe, some 1,400 North Carolinians took part in the battle. Because of their inability to invade the South, the British once again turned their attention to the North. It would be almost four years before North Carolina would know the tramp of British boots, the stench of burnt gunpowder, and sting of British musketry.

1776 July 25

Having received news of the Declaration of Independence three days earlier, the Provincial Council of Safety adopted a resolution absolving North Carolinians of "all Allegiance to the British Crown." The council then ordered the safety committees of the counties and towns to proclaim America's independence. On August 1, 1776, Cornelius Harnett, president of the Council of Safety, read publicly for the first time in North Carolina the Declaration of Independence. The Halifax crowd enthusiastically hailed the Continental Congress's proclamation which broke the ties with the mother country.

1776 August 9

The Declaration of Independence and the urgings of the Continental Congress to draft state constitutions prompted the Council of Safety to order elections on October 15. North Carolinians were to elect delegates to a Fifth Provincial Congress at Halifax for the purpose of establishing a state government and drawing up a state constitution. Asserting that the new government should be "fixed and Permanent," the council asked citizens to choose their representatives wisely and carefully, for the nature of the government formed would determine "the happiness or Misery of the State."

1776 October 15

The election campaign for the Fifth Provincial Congress proved to be exciting and acrimonious. The whig forces, once unified in the movement for independence, had ruptured over the nature of the new government. The conservative faction desired a government that differed little from its royal predecessor. Led by Samuel Johnston, James Iredell, and William Hooper, among others, the conservatives insisted on a strong executive, an independent judiciary with life tenure, the protection of property rights, and property qualifications which tended to limit suffrage and officeholding. Perhaps Johnston stated the conservative position most aptly when he declared that he had no confidence in "numbers."

Arrayed against the conservatives were the so-called radicals, led by Willie Jones, Griffith Rutherford, and Thomas Person, a former regulator. The radicals stood for what they termed a "simple democracy" with a strong legislature, weak executive, and religious freedom from an established church.

In a campaign marked by vituperation and violence, Samuel Johnston became the object of the radicals' wrath. Burned in effigy and defeated at the polls, Johnston later complained: "Everyone who has the least pretensions to be a gentleman is borne down *per ignobile vulgus*—a set of men without reading, experience, or principles to govern them."

Amid charges of "fraud and debauchery," some 169 delegates representing thirty-two counties and nine towns were elected. The Fifth Provincial Congress would hold about an equal number of radicals and conservatives; the so-called moderates would exercise the balance of power.

Samuel Johnston

Willie Jones

1776 November 12

Lasting nearly six weeks, the Fifth Provincial Congress drafted a state constitution, formulated a bill of rights, and established North Carolina's first state government. Adopting a significant new procedure, the Halifax Congress decided to vote by "voice" rather than by town or county, thereby instituting majority rule. Richard Caswell, the hero of the Battle of Moore's Creek Bridge, was unanimously elected president of the convention.

The Declaration of Rights, adopted on December 17, 1776, consisted of twenty-five articles which safeguarded the rights of the people against oppressive government and drew heavily upon past precedents such as the Magna Carta (1215) and English Bill of Rights (1689). The Constitution enacted on December 18, 1776, provided for popular sovereignty, separation of powers, and three branches of government.

Rooted in the colonial experience, the new constitution guaranteed elections, the precedence of civil over military power, the right of assembly, and freedom from arbitrary taxation. The legislative branch was to be bicameral with members of each house chosen in annual elections. While property qualifications for the senate were slightly higher than those for the lower house, the suffrage, based on landholding or the ability to pay "public taxes," was extended to all "freemen," white or black. Vested with control of the executive branch, the General Assembly was empowered to elect the governor, council of state, attorney general, and other executive officers each year. The governor was only eligible to hold office three out of any six successive years. By a joint ballot, the General Assembly also had the power to elect judges of the state Supreme Court. In addition the legislature chose delegates to the Continental Congress.

Although the North Carolina Constitution of 1776 reflected both the former colonial government and the colonial experience, there were changes too. Most importantly, power had shifted away from the executive and to the legislature. The governor, in contrast to royal executives, was denied the power to call elections, to summon, prorogue, or dissolve the General Assembly, or to veto legislation. The legislature exercised further control over the executive by annual elections and short terms of office. In a sense, the radicals had secured the form if not substance of the government they sought.

But the conservatives were not without their victories as well. There were property qualifications for suffrage and officeholding as well as religious disqualifications which peremptorily denied officeholding to non-Protestants. As in other states, the new constitution was not submitted to the citizenry for a popular vote. Finally, the new instrument of government lacked one essential power, a deficiency which would generate much controversy during the next sixty years — the power of amendment had been omitted.

In comparison with other state constitutions drawn up during the American Revolution, the North Carolina document most resembled the Virginia and Maryland constitutions. Even so, North Carolina in its constitution of 1776 made a broader commitment to representative government than many other states in the forefront of the revolutionary movement.

1776 December 23

Having completed its assigned duties, the Fifth and last Provincial Congress adjourned after electing Richard Caswell to be the state's first governor. Caswell immediately assumed his office as interim governor until the first state legislature could meet and elect a chief executive.

1777 April 7

The state's first General Assembly convened on this date. Procedural questions characterized the lawmakers' early deliberations, but more substantive issues demanded action as well. By a joint ballot the two houses unanimously elected Richard Caswell governor, a position he continued to hold for the next three years. The legislature also passed acts providing for loyalty oaths, the confiscation of tory property, and poll taxes. Having elected a governor and council of state, the assemblymen named Thomas Burke, John Penn, and Cornelius Harnett delegates to the Continental Congress. One notable statute was an "Act to prevent domestic Insurrections." There had been several instances of Quakers manumitting their slaves at a time when the British were offering slaves their freedom for remaining loyal to the crown. Believing the Quakers' action dangerous to the state's security, the lawmakers declared that henceforth no slave could be freed except for "meritorious Services" which were to be judged by a county court.

The General Assembly's basic worry, however, continued to be military preparedness. Fearing a renewal of Indian warfare on the frontier, the legislature extended the length of service of the militia under Griffith Rutherford. In addition the lawmakers decided to send North Carolina's Continental Line north to join General George Washington. As a result, North Carolina continentals saw action at Brandywine and Germantown in 1777 and at the Battle of Monmouth in 1778. Even more dramatically, hundreds of North Carolinians suffered through the bitter winter of 1777-1778 at Valley Forge with little food, shelter, or clothing. Since 1776, North Carolina had been spared the misery of war on its own soil, but an end to that interlude was fast approaching.

1777 July 20

During the summer of 1776 Griffith Rutherford had waged a campaign against the Cherokees in the western part of the state. The Cherokees, it was believed, were being inflamed by British agents and traders. Rutherford's offensive had devastated a large portion of the "Indian country." Led by the elderly chief Attakullakulla (Little Carpenter), the Cherokees signed the Treaty of Long Island (in the Holston River) which ceded to whites all the lands east of the Blue Ridge Mountains and various rivers. By this treaty, it was hoped that the Indian threat on the frontier might be quelled.

1778 April 24

The North Carolina General Assembly ratified the Articles of Confederation which eventually provided the first federal government for the nation. The Articles did not go into effect, however, until 1781 when the final reluctant states ratified them. In the Continental Congress John Penn and Cornelius Harnett had supported the Articles, but Thomas Burke had opposed them. Burke, a sturdy advocate of state's rights, shared with many other whigs a distrust of federal, congressional, and executive power. He plainly stated that position in a letter to Governor Caswell in 1778. "The rights of private citizens," Burke asserted, "and even of our sovereign communities are at present so little regarded in Congress that any rumor will determine a majority to violate both and it is hardly safe to oppose it, [for] every argument against the unlimited power of Congress to judge of necessity, and under the idea to interpose with Military force is heard with great reluctance, hardly with patience, and the internal police and sovereignty of States, are treated as chimerical phantoms." When Burke's term expired, he refused to be considered for reelection and temporarily retired.

Robert Howe

1778 December 29

The pall of war hung heavy over the South. Having failed to conquer Washington's army in the North, Sir Henry Clinton determined to invade the South in hopes of stirring loyalist sentiment which was known to be strong in the Carolinas. On this date the British captured Savannah and rapidly swept through Georgia, thereby restoring royal rule. General Robert Howe of North Carolina, commanding officer of the Southern Department, was blamed for the defeat at Savannah and court-martialed. Though subsequently acquitted "with the Highest Honor," Howe lost his command but remained active in the Continental Army.

1779 January 19

The North Carolina legislature met for the first of a number of sessions during the year. While military preparations dominated legislative concerns with the British again in the South, the lawmakers also felt threatened internally by dissenting elements. In 1779 the legislature adopted a severe Confiscation Act which not only permitted the seizure of loyalist property but also listed a large number of prominent tories including William Tryon, Josiah Martin, Edmund Fanning, Sir Nathaniel Duckinfield, Henry E. McCulloh, and others. Most conservatives in the General Assembly objected to the law, but the radicals, with the notable exceptions of Willie Jones and Timothy Bloodworth, insisted on the harsh measures. The statute enabled the state to receive vast sums of money from the sale of tory property, and it had the concomitant effect of redistributing property, although not necessarily among small landholders.

The General Assembly also considered measures to deal with dissenting religious sects. One proposal was an oath to be administered to all Quakers, Moravians, Mennonites, and Dunkards. By promising their fidelity to the state of North Carolina, they were to deny assistance to the British and to report any and all conspiracies directed against the whig government. Such a pledge, however, proved ineffectual since these religious sects forbade the swearing of oaths.

Even so, the legislature instituted a new policy in regard to taxation and military duty. Previously, pacifist sects such as the Quakers and Moravians had been obliged to pay for substitutes if they refused conscription into the Continental Army. Under a new act, the members of those sects were exempted from military service but required to pay a threefold tax. In other words, the amount of their *ad valorem* and tax-in-kind assessments were thereafter multiplied by three. The policy continued during the rest of the war.

An Act for Confiscating the Property of all such persons as are Inimical to the United States, and of such persons as shall not within a certain time therein mentioned appear and submit to this State whether they shall be received as Citizens thereof, and of such persons as shall thereafter have arms and shall not be admitted as Citizens, and for other purposes therein mentioned

Whereas divers persons who have heretofore owned and possessed Lands, Tenements, and Hereditaments, and also moveable Property in this State, have withdrawn themselves from the same, and attached themselves to the Enemies of the United States of America, and also divers persons have withdrawn to places beyond the bounds of any of the United States, in order to avoid bearing their just and equal part in defence of the Freedom and Independency of the same; and also divers persons, who having been beyond the bounds of the same United States at the beginning of the present War, have failed to return and unite their Efforts for the Common defence of America's Liberties; and it is expedient and just that every person, for whose safety is protected in any State, should be and ought to bear within the same, or join in defence thereof whenever the same is threatened or invaded; and it is also just that a reasonable time be given for such as have it in their power to allege favorable or mitigating circumstances, to induce this State, ever attentive to the rights of National Justice and ever ready and willing to receive to Grace and favour all who are sincerely attached to Liberty, to receive them as Citizens, and restore them to the Possessions which once belonged to them:

44

Confiscation Act

1780 April 17

When the legislature assembled in April, 1780, renewed armed conflict in North Carolina appeared imminent. Determined to provide the best defense possible for the state, the lawmakers appointed Richard Caswell major general of the entire state militia. Under the constitution Caswell, who had served three successive terms, was no longer eligible for the governorship. Abner Nash of New Bern became the new governor.

Familiar problems continued to plague the assembly. Because the religious dissenters would not take the loyalty oath, zealous whigs were attempting to seize their property. Under the act of 1777 requiring an oath of allegiance, those who refused the pledge had no legal recourse to protect themselves or their property. The legislature thus gave the religious dissenters special relief from the provisions of the former law.

Financially the state still stood on shaky ground. Lacking specie, credit, and the necessary revenue to fund the state's currency, the legislature had resorted to fiat money. In 1780, the lawmakers ordered the emission of another $850,000 in currency and postponed for another year the redemption of a similar issuance made in 1776. The fiat money only fueled the already rampant inflation. Embarrassed by the state's empty treasury, and feeling a strong moral and legal obligation to the North Carolina continentals, the General Assembly also passed the so-called "Bonus Act of 1780" which set aside a military reservation for the state's veterans. Supplemented by another act two years later, the military reservation provided land grants of up to 640 acres for each veteran.

1780 May 12

The Southern Department of the Continental Army consisted of some 7,000 troops, of whom about 2,000 were North Carolinians. At times, as many as 1,500 North Carolina militiamen were attached to the Continental Line. These troops formed the bulwark of North Carolina's defense against the British who, having taken Georgia, were now sweeping through South Carolina.

At Charleston in May, 1780, the British inflicted a devastating defeat on the Americans under the command of General Benjamin Lincoln. Two brigades from the North Carolina Line and 1,000 North Carolina militiamen took part in the battle. In a stunning British victory, over 800 North Carolina continentals and 600 militiamen were captured. The loss of Charleston boded ill, for now Lord Charles Cornwallis stood poised to invade North Carolina and Virginia.

1780 June 20

With the approach of an invading British army from the south, civil war between whig and tory forces broke out along the North Carolina border. At Ramsour's Mill a whig force of some 400 men defeated a tory force over twice its size. Similarly, small bands of whig partisans won victories at Hanging Rock in South Carolina and Colson's Mill on the Pee Dee River in July. These small but important engagements helped to undermine the tory cause in North Carolina, disrupt British military movements, and raise confidence in the fighting efficacy of militia units.

1780 July 25

General Horatio Gates, regarded by some as the hero of Saratoga, received command of the Southern Department at Hillsborough. Gates succeeded Benjamin Lincoln, now a prisoner of war in Charleston. Gates's new command included 3,000 continentals and 1,200 North Carolina militia, the latter led by Richard Caswell and Griffith Rutherford.

1780 August 16

Despite warnings from his subordinates, Gates impulsively marched into South Carolina to engage the British. At the Battle of Camden, Lord Cornwallis routed the American army in an ignominious defeat that cost the patriots 800 killed and

1,000 captured—including Griffith Rutherford—out of a force numbering over 3,000. About one-half of the dead were North Carolinians. Gates and Caswell eluded capture and made their way to Charlotte. From there Gates continued his flight all the way to Hillsborough in the remarkable space of three days. For the debacle at Camden, Gates was relieved of his command. Because his militiamen had broken ranks early in the battle and fled in terror, Caswell was removed as commanding officer of the North Carolina militia. The embittered Caswell resigned from the militia, though he later returned to public service as a member of the Council Extraordinary which oversaw military affairs.

1780 August 23

The defeat at Camden left North Carolina perilously vulnerable to Cornwallis's pending invasion. With the state on the verge of panic, Governor Abner Nash reported to the General Assembly that the Council of State had refused to attend sessions or assist him in the conduct of the war. He asked that a Board of War be instituted to advise him on military matters when the assembly was not in session. Nash argued that such a board was necessary for the defense of "our lives, liberties and fortunes."

1780 September 12

In compliance with the governor's wishes, the legislature established a Board of War consisting of three members— Alexander Martin, John Penn, and Oroondates Davis. The board created more problems than it solved, however. Penn took an active role in controlling the military operations of the state's troops, much to the displeasure and chagrin of the governor. Charging that the Board of War had exercised powers "superceeding those of the Executive," Nash threatened to resign unless his powers were restored. Though he ascribed no sinister motive to Penn's activities, Nash genuinely believed that a dangerous usurpation of the constitution had taken place; so he demanded the abolition of the board. The legislature agreed, for in January, 1781, it annulled the Board of War and replaced it with a Council Extraordinary consisting of Richard Caswell, Alexander Martin, and Allen Jones.

John Penn

1780 September 26

After Camden, Cornwallis made a slow and harassed march to Charlotte. North Carolina partisans, led by William R. Davie and William L. Davidson, proved quite nettlesome to the British. The whig forces managed to keep Cornwallis's army isolated by cutting off communications between the British and loyalists in other parts of the state. Although he had planned to fortify the town and enlist tory volunteers, Cornwallis found Charlotte inhospitable since it sat "in a d----d rebellious country."

1780 October 3

Josiah Martin, the former royal governor, issued a proclamation announcing a British victory and the restoration of the crown's sovereignty in North Carolina since Cornwallis had occupied Charlotte. The American victory at King's Mountain on October 7, however, convinced Cornwallis otherwise, and he retreated into South Carolina once again.

1780 October 7

The Battle of King's Mountain was a magnificent victory for the "over-mountain men." Cornwallis had dispatched Colonel Patrick Ferguson to protect his left flank as he drove northward into North Carolina. At Gilbert Town in Rutherford County, Ferguson had imperiously announced that if the mountain patriots did not lay down their arms, "he would march his forces over the mountains, hang their leaders, and lay waste to their country with fire and sword."

In response to the impudent threat, frontiersmen from Virginia, North Carolina, South Carolina, Georgia, and what later became Tennessee joined forces to attack the British army. Ferguson retreated to King's Mountain and camped atop its steep slopes, some one-and-one-half miles from the North Carolina border. In a brilliant four-pronged attack, the undisciplined and untrained militia captured the mountain while inflicting heavy losses on the enemy. Ferguson was killed. The victory was all the more remarkable because the military force had proceeded without the leadership or guidance of the state or of the Continental Line.

The year 1780 had been a gloomy one indeed for the whig cause, but this victory revived waning spirits. Sir Henry Clinton termed it a "fatal catastrophe." With his left flank now unguarded, and his confidence in North Carolina loyalism shaken, Cornwallis speedily retreated from Charlotte to Winnsboro, South Carolina.

1780 December 2

Nathanael Greene, one of Washington's ablest generals, took command of the Southern Department at Charlotte. In the wake of Gates's disastrous defeat at Camden, the strength of the army had fallen to only 2,300 men, with perhaps no more than a third of them fit for military service. Many were untrained militia; others lacked arms and clothing. Nevertheless, Greene had a brilliant cadre of officers including Count

Kosciusko, Daniel Morgan, and "Light Horse Harry" Lee. William R. Davie, the youthful North Carolinian, became Greene's commissary officer.

1781 January 17

Daniel Morgan with 1,000 men, 300 of whom were North Carolinians, defeated Colonel Banastre Tarleton at Cowpens on the Broad River. Both Cornwallis and Greene had divided their armies before the engagement at Cowpens. Maddened by his able subaltern's defeat, Cornwallis began a hot pursuit of Morgan, who retreated toward Charlotte. When Greene learned of Cornwallis's movement, he assumed command of Morgan's forces. The rest of his army under Issac Huger he sent northward toward Salisbury or Guilford Court House.

The stage was now set for Greene's masterly retreat across the rolling hills of the North Carolina Piedmont. Closely behind him trailed Cornwallis with an army of 3,000 seasoned British soldiers.

1781 February 13

For three weeks Greene skillfully eluded Cornwallis, who remained some twenty-five miles behind the American forces. Despite the swollen condition of the Catawba and Yadkin, Greene negotiated the rivers in the dead of winter. A cold, relentless rain hampered the operations of both armies. Cornwallis burned as much of his excess baggage as he dared in order to gain on the wily Greene. On this date the Quaker general finally crossed the Dan River into Virginia. Tired of the frustrating chase, Cornwallis repaired to Hillsborough. Issuing a proclamation, Cornwallis asserted that he had come to North Carolina to rescue the king's loyal subjects.

In fact, Greene had reunited his army, drawn Cornwallis 230 miles from his base of supply, and left the British army in whig country with sparse provisions in mid-winter. Moreover, Greene's tactical retreat spurred new enthusiasm as recruits poured into his army and swelled ranks to over 4,000.

Nathanael Greene

Lord Charles Cornwallis

Now heavily reinforced, Greene crossed back into North Carolina as Cornwallis advanced to engage him. They met at Guilford Court House in a ferocious battle. Cornwallis supposedly said in tribute to the Continental Army, "The Americans fought like demons." The North Carolina militia, which suffered a number of lost or wounded, formed the first two lines of defense against the British assault.

Though Cornwallis held the field, Greene exacted heavy losses that badly weakened the British army. Cornwallis's situation provoked the famous statement by British politician Charles

The Cavalry Charge—The Battle of Guilford Court House

James Fox that, "Another such victory would destroy the British army." Indeed, the Battle of Guilford Court House left Cornwallis in an untenable position logistically and militarily.

Too weakened to assume the offensive once again, Cornwallis proclaimed a victory over Greene, the restoration of royal rule, and pardons for all rebels who laid down their arms. He then marched to Wilmington, which had recently succumbed to British control, in order to rest and replenish his army. The march proceeded slowly, and Cornwallis did not arrive in the port city until April 7.

The Marches of Lord Cornwallis

1781 April 25

Exasperated that Greene had refused to pursue him, Cornwallis decided to invade Virginia. To do otherwise would have been to admit failure. Greene, after leaving Guilford Court House, had ignored Cornwallis and instead retaken backcountry posts at Camden, Ninety-Six, and Augusta, thereby leaving the British with only the port cities of Wilmington, Charleston, and Savannah in the entire South.

It was now evident that Cornwallis had not conquered North and South Carolina at all. In fact, the British appeared to be in a weaker position than before his long campaign. After announcing the conquest of North Carolina and the restoration of

Governor Josiah Martin for yet another time, Cornwallis left Wilmington on this date and hastened to his fate at Yorktown, where he surrendered on October 19. The British evacuated Wilmington on November 18. The departure of British soldiers from North Carolina, however, did not signal the end of bloodshed and warfare as events during the following months cruelly demonstrated.

1781 September 12

On this date David Fanning led a group of some 950 tories in a surprise attack on Hillsborough. In suffering only one wounded, Fanning, a notorious cutthroat in whig eyes, killed fifteen patriots, wounded twenty, and took over 200 prisoners including Governor Thomas Burke, his council, a number of army officers, and seventy-one Continental soldiers.

Fanning's bold raid marked an amazing victory for the loyalists who immediately marched to Wilmington with their prisoners. Governor Burke was imprisoned at the port city until November when he was paroled to James Island. On January 16, 1782, North Carolina's governor broke his "parole" and fled to freedom to resume his executive duties.

Fanning's escapades illustrated only part of a larger pattern of civil warfare, known as the "Tory War," that continued unabated between loyalists and whigs during 1781 and 1782. Though Fanning had earned his reputation of carnage and bloodshed, whig atrocities were not unknown. Peace continued to evade war-weary North Carolinians.

1782 April 16

In a message to the General Assembly, Governor Burke warned that critical days still lay ahead for North Carolina. The war with Great Britain had ended, but the revolution, according to some, had scarcely begun. Political acrimony, economic difficulties, and social unrest continued to afflict the

David Fanning Flees

Tories Hanged in Effigy

state. Burke's message evidenced his concern for these problems. The governor condemned the inefficiency of local government, the feckless judicial system, and the incompetence of many officeholders. Urging the legislature to enact constructive measures to alleviate these problems, Burke cautioned: "While our Arms are [still] prevailing is therefore the precise season for such actions as remain to put us in possession of peace and prosperity."

1782 May 7

No longer able to tolerate the bloodshed and fighting, David Fanning departed North Carolina and went to a truce area in South Carolina. He later traveled to Charleston and subsequently in 1784 on to Halifax, Nova Scotia.

Fanning's flight brought to an end the brutal civil war in North Carolina between tories and whigs. Arson, pillaging, and murder—seemingly without compunction—had terrorized North Carolinians for nearly two years. Fanning's marauding activities stamped him as the bête noire of the revolutionary period in North Carolina.

1783 April 18

Meeting in April, 1783, the General Assembly made a gesture toward pardoning loyalists. In the "Act of Pardon and Oblivion," the lawmakers offered amnesty to all tories, save five classes—those who held commissions in the British army; those sixty-eight men named in the Confiscation Act of 1779; those absent from the state during the previous twelve months; those guilty of murder, rape, robbery, or arson; and despised loyalists like David Fanning.

Hundreds of tories fled the state during the war and afterward as petitions for the return of their property were ignored. The Treaty of Paris (1783) between the United States and Great Britain notwithstanding, the state government continued to sell confiscated loyalist property as late as 1790.

The Cession Act by the state legislature set in motion a strange series of events that briefly led to the formation of the state of Franklin. Convening in April, 1784, the General Assembly agreed to cede the state's western lands to the federal government. The grant of land was to be used by all the states.

Strong opposition to the measure, however, existed in the legislature. Led by William R. Davie, opponents of the Cession Act argued that the western lands should be sold to help liquidate the state's debt. That faction eventually prevailed, for in October, 1784, the legislature repealed the act by a large margin.

John Sevier

The Cession Act, nonetheless, was quite popular in the western counties. Settlers in that region believed that state government had ignored them since it had provided inadequate military protection from the Indians. Nor were there any courts west of Morganton which sat on the eastern slopes of the Blue Ridge. The transmontane settlers suffered genuine hardships.

In August, 1784, a convention of frontiersmen met in Jonesborough, and, led by John Sevier — a Revolutionary War hero — it urged the Continental Congress to accept North Carolina's cession. In December, 1784, four of the transmontane counties went a step farther by declaring independence from North Carolina and adopting a provisional constitution similar to North Carolina's.

For the next several years a quasi-state, known as Franklin, attempted to act independently of North Carolina. In 1785 Franklin's legislature elected John Sevier governor and justified separation from North Carolina on the grounds of unjust taxation, the alleged anti-western animus of eastern North Carolinians, and the failure of the mother state to compensate the Indians for lands taken from them. A delegate was even sent to the Continental Congress, but the Congress refused to recognize him since North Carolina had revoked the Cession Act.

Meanwhile, Governor Alexander Martin issued a "Manifesto" denouncing the state of Franklin and warning the western settlers that they risked civil war. In July, 1788, provoked by Sevier's attacks on Indians, and alarmed by a clash between Sevier's followers and the state militia, Governor Samuel Johnston ordered the arrest of Franklin's bold leader. Held only temporarily, Sevier acceded to the sovereignty of North Carolina and won election to the state assembly in 1789.

The independent state of Franklin collapsed. North Carolina eventually ceded its western lands to the United States in 1789 from which the new state of Tennessee was carved in 1796.

1784 April

The Confiscation Acts directed against loyalists have often been interpreted as blows for social democracy since they tended to redistribute property. In fact, the Confiscation Acts were primarily military measures designed to promote internal security by demoralizing and debilitating the tories.

Nonetheless, after the war the North Carolina legislature did take steps to enlarge the opportunity to acquire and hold real property by abolishing entail and primogeniture. A 1784 law promised to "promote that equality of property which is of the spirit and principle of a genuine republic." Estates of persons dying intestate, according to the statute, must "undergo a more general and equal distribution." Thereafter, such estates were to be divided equally among all sons instead of passing wholly to the eldest. If there were no sons, then the daughters became the legatees. Though North Carolina was not the only state to abolish entail and primogeniture, the law bespoke the strong democratic undercurrent that had helped shape the Revolution.

1786 July 10

The sharp factional disputes that had rent the whigs in the 1770s did not cease during the 1780s but merely intensified. The radical whigs had won "their war" in a sense. Legislative powers had been preserved and expanded often at the expense of executive authority. More importantly, the Articles of Confederation provided a federal government so weak and so decentralized that it had no power to tax and depended on a requisition system from the states just to operate.

During the 1780s, a group of energetic "nationalists" worked sedulously to change the Articles and to institute a stronger central government. Led by such luminaries as Alexander Hamilton of New York, James Madison and George Washington of Virginia, and Robert Morris of Pennsylvania, the nationalists argued for a federal government with independent revenue and executive leadership. For a variety of reasons, these nationalists perceived internal and external threats to the United States if an enfeebled federal government persisted.

In 1786 Alexander Hamilton and other nationalists called for a convention of all the states at Annapolis, Maryland, ostensibly to consider trade problems and the commercial interests of the United States. Responding to the request in July, 1786, Governor Richard Caswell appointed Abner Nash, Alfred

Moore, Hugh Williamson, John Gray Blount, and Philemon Hawkins to represent North Carolina at Annapolis. Not every state sent delegates, but the Annapolis meeting proved to be a rehearsal for the Constitutional Convention in Philadelphia the following year. Hugh Williamson, the only North Carolina delegate who tried to reach Annapolis, arrived a day after the convention had adjourned.

1787 January 6

On the last day of the General Assembly, the lawmakers elected William R. Davie, Richard Dobbs Spaight, Governor Richard Caswell, Alexander Martin, and Willie Jones to the Constitutional Convention in Philadelphia. Hugh Williamson and William Blount later replaced Jones and Caswell who decided not to accept the appointment.

North Carolina had taken no lead in the movement for an invigorated central government or the calling of a constitutional convention. Most North Carolinians were yeomen farmers who owned small tracts of land and few slaves, if any. Tending toward radical whiggery, they opposed strong governments and maintained control of the state assembly during most years. North Carolina had a well-deserved reputation for staunch antifederalism

But there were nationalists, or Federalists as they were becoming known, in North Carolina too. The delegates to the Philadelphia convention exemplified the Federalist tradition in the state. They were wealthy planters or businessmen generally from the eastern part of the state. Conservative in political, social, and economic outlook, they represented the ruling elite of the state.

1787 October 4

The *State Gazette of North Carolina* published for the first time in North Carolina the Constitution adopted in Philadelphia. The Constitution's publication signaled the beginning of a bitter struggle between Federalists and Antifederalists over ratification which would continue for the next two years.

Hugh Williamson

William Blount

Alexander Martin

Richard Dobbs Spaight

William Richardson Davie

North Carolina's Delegates to the Constitutional Convention

1787 November

In a landmark decision—*Bayard v. Singleton*—a North Carolina court overturned a law and declared it unconstitutional. Under a 1785 statute which was based on the Confiscation Acts, loyalists had been prohibited from bringing suits against persons who now possessed their property. Judges Samuel Ashe, Samuel Spencer, and John Williams ruled that the 1785 law deprived a citizen of his property without a jury trial, and thus the statute was unconstitutional.

This case marked the first time that a North Carolina court exercised judicial review under a written constitution. The decision was an early precedent for Chief Justice John Marshall's ruling in *Marbury v. Madison* by the United States Supreme Court in 1803.

1787 December 6

The state legislature met and called for an election of five delegates from each county and one from each borough town for a convention to consider ratification of the federal Constitution. The campaign that followed pitted suspicious Antifederalists against resolute Federalists. Character assassination, violence, and fraud marred the election. Antifederalist Thomas Person branded George Washington a "damned rascal and traitor to his country," while Federalist Archibald Maclaine compared the opposition to "a set of fools and Knaves."

The Antifederalists won a sweeping victory by a margin of 184 delegates to 83 for the Federalists. Among the Federalist casualties in the election were William Hooper, whose eye had been blackened by an Antifederalist during the campaign, Richard Caswell, and Alfred Moore.

1787 December 22

The General Assembly passed a statute declaring the Treaty of Paris (1783) to be the law of the land and ordering the North Carolina courts to recognize the treaty and "to judge accordingly." If truly enforced, the act promised to end all discrimination against loyalists.

1788 July 21

North Carolina's ratification convention met in Hillsborough. Though the Antifederalists had a vast majority, they voted with the Federalists to elect Governor Samuel Johnston president of the convention. Led by Willie Jones, Timothy Bloodworth, Thomas Person, and others, the Antifederalists objected to the Constitution because it lacked sufficient safeguards for state's rights and civil liberties. Until a bill of rights was presented to the state, the Antifederalists argued, North Carolina would continue to oppose ratification. James Iredell and William R. Davie presented the Federalist case for ratification. After eleven days of debate, the convention voted 184 to 83 not to ratify the Constitution at that time.

Eleven other states had already given their consent to the implementation of the Constitution, two more than necessary. Now only North Carolina and Rhode Island stood outside the Union as sovereign and independent states.

1789 November 21

Assembling in Fayetteville, a second ratifying convention approved the Constitution by a vote of 195 to 77. What had happened in the intervening year to reverse public opinion so overwhelmingly?

Part of the answer lay in the effective propaganda campaign waged by Iredell and Davie since 1788. Too, economic prosperity had returned after the depression years of 1785 and 1786, and there was a growing public discontent with the continued emission of paper money by the Antifederalist-dominated legislatures. Moreover, outside the Union, North Carolina would be liable to federal tariffs and tonnage duties, an unhappy prospect. Finally, James Madison had taken the lead in the House of Representatives to draft a bill of rights which would amend the Constitution. His proposal had been submitted to the states in September, 1789.

Each of these reasons singularly may not have been enough to prompt ratification, but in concert they provided persuasive and compelling evidence for adoption of the Constitution. Thus, North Carolina joined the United States even before the first ten amendments had been ratified.

James Iredell, Appointed Justice of the United States Supreme Court by President George Washington

BIBLIOGRAPHICAL SOURCES

Butler, Lindley S. "The Coming of the Revolution in North Carolina, 1760-1776," unpublished doctoral dissertation, University of North Carolina, Chapel Hill, 1971.

Clark, Walter, ed. *The State Records of North Carolina.* 16 vols. Winston and Goldsboro: State of North Carolina, 1895-1907.

DeMond, Robert O. *The Loyalists in North Carolina During the Revolution.* Durham: Duke University Press, 1940.

Dill, Alonzo T. *Governor Tryon and His Palace.* Chapel Hill: University of North Carolina Press, 1955.

Ganyard, Robert L. "North Carolina During the American Revolution: The First Phase, 1774-1777," unpublished doctoral dissertation, Duke University, 1962.

Greene, Jack P. *The Quest for Power: The Lower Houses of Assembly in the Southern Royal Colonies, 1689-1776.* Chapel Hill: University of North Carolina Press, 1963.

Koesy, Sheldon F. "Continuity and Change in North Carolina, 1775-1789," unpublished doctoral dissertation, Duke University, 1963.

Lefler, Hugh T. and Newsome, Albert R. *North Carolina: The History of a Southern State.* Third Edition. Chapel Hill: University of North Carolina Press, 1973.

Lefler, Hugh T. and Powell, William S. *Colonial North Carolina: A History.* New York: Charles Scribner's Sons, 1973.

Rankin, Hugh F. *The North Carolina Continentals.* Chapel Hill: University of North Carolina Press, 1971.

Robinson, Blackwell P. *William R. Davie.* Chapel Hill: University of North Carolina Press, 1957.

Saunders, William L., ed. *The Colonial Records of North Carolina.* 10 vols. Raleigh: State of North Carolina, 1886-1890.

Sellers, Charles G., Jr. "Making a Revolution: The North Carolina Whigs, 1765-1775," in J. C. Sitterson, ed., *Studies in Southern History.* Chapel Hill: University of North Carolina Press, 1957.

Troxler, George W. "The Homefront in Revolutionary North Carolina," unpublished doctoral dissertation, University of North Carolina, Chapel Hill, 1970.